What is a force?

Jacqui Bailey

A⁺
Smart Apple Media

First published in 2005 by Franklin Watts
96 Leonard Street, London EC2A 4XD

Franklin Watts Australia
45-51 Huntley Street, Alexandria, NSW 2015

Series editor: Rachel Cooke, **Editor:** Jennifer Schofield, **Design:** Rachel Hamdi/Holly Mann, **Picture researcher:** Diana Morris, **Photography:** Ray Moller, unless otherwise acknowledged

Acknowledgements:
Tom Brakefield/Image Works/Topham: 28b. NASA: 29b. Powell/Topham: 15b.

Published in the United States by Smart Apple Media
2140 Howard Drive West, North Mankato, Minnesota 56003

Library of Congress Cataloging-in-Publication Data

Bailey, Jacqui.
What is a force? / by Jacqui Bailey.
p. cm. — (Investigating science)
ISBN-13 : 978-1-58340-925-1
Includes index.
1. Force and energy—Juvenile literature. I. Title.

QC73.4.B35 2006
531'.6—dc22   2005052293

9 8 7 6 5 4 3 2 1

Contents

On the move

Look around you. What can you see that moves?

THINK about all of the different ways things move.

● Balls bounce, marbles roll, cars race, windmills whirl, and cranes lift.

● Animals stretch, run, climb, crawl, swim, fly, hop, and wriggle.

What about you? How many **movements** can you make?

You will need:

A sheet of paper (lined, if possible) ✔

A pencil and a ruler ✔

Space to jump around! ✔

How many ways can you move?

1. Use the pencil and ruler to draw a line down the middle of the paper.

2. In the left-hand column, list all the movements you can think of.

3 Try to do all the movements on your list. In the right-hand column, check off each one as you do it.

4 See what movements your friends can make.

Because . . .

*We can move in so many ways because of the **joints** and **muscles** in our bodies. Joints link our bones together like hinges. Muscles pull on the bones and make them move at the joints. Our muscles are using a **force** to make us move.*

Push and pull

Everything needs a force to make it move. Although you cannot see a force, you can see what it does. A force is either a push or a pull.

THINK about what happens when you push or pull something.
- You pull open a drawer.
- You push away a soccer ball with a kick.
- You lift a wheelbarrow with a pull and then push it along.

Try moving some other things. Do you use pushes or pulls?

You will need:

A sheet of paper (lined, if possible) ✔

A pencil and a ruler ✔

A group of objects (e.g. a toy car, a bouncy ball, a roll of tape, a marble, an eraser, a drink with a straw in it, a pencil) ✔

How do you make things move?

1. Divide your paper into two columns with a line down the middle.

2. Write the word "push" at the top of one column and "pull" at the top of the other.

3. Look at your objects and choose the best way to move each one—with a push or a pull. Write the name of the object in the column with that heading.

4. Now make the objects move and find out if you were right.

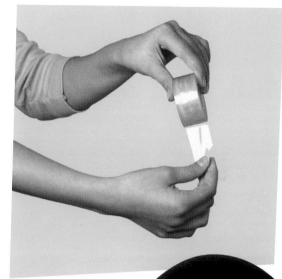

Because . . .

All of the objects move because of a push or a pull. Pushing something moves it away from you, pulling something moves it toward you. For example, sucking a drink through a straw pulls the liquid toward your mouth.

Big push, little push

We can make things move with a big force
or a small one.

THINK about what happens when
you push a friend on a swing.

- A small push makes the
swing move a little.
- A big push makes the
swing move a lot.

So, how does the
strength of a force
change the way an
object moves?

Try pushing some
coins to find out.

You will need:

A piece of paper about 12 inches
(30 cm) by 18 inches (45 cm) ✔

A pencil and a ruler ✔

A large board or table top ✔

Tape ✔

3 large coins of the same size ✔

Which force moves a coin the most?

1 Use the ruler to mark every 4 inches (10 cm) down both sides of the sheet of paper. Draw lines to connect each pair of marks and number each line.

2 Lay the paper flat on the board or table top, so its top end lies along one edge. Tape it firmly in position.

3 Place a coin on the top edge of the paper so it juts out a little over the side.

4 Give the coin a push with your hand. How far can you make it slide along the paper? What happens if you push the next coin harder, or less hard?

Because . . .

A big push makes a coin travel farther than a small push. This is because the greater the force used on an object, the more it moves. The same is true of pulling. You can see how this works when you pull on an elastic band.

Heavy and light

A light object is easy to move.
It can be hard to move a
heavy object.

THINK about the amount
of force you need to move
a heavy object or a light one.

- Can you throw a
  basketball as far as you
  can throw a tennis ball?
  Does it take more or
  less force?

  - Is it easier to
    move a chair or
    a table? Which is
    heavier?

  Investigate how
  much force you use
  to move a box.

You will need:

2 strips of paper ✔

A large cardboard box ✔

A pile of soft cushions ✔

A pile of books ✔

Which box takes the most force to move?

1 Put the strips of paper on the floor, 10 feet (3 m) apart, to make a start and a finish line.

2 Put the empty box in front of one line and push or pull it to the other line. How much force did you need?

3 Fill the cardboard box with cushions and push or pull it back to the start line. Was it easier or harder this time?

4 Now fill the box with books. How much force does it take to push or pull it between the lines? (If you cannot move the box at all, take out books until you can.)

Because . . .

The box of books took the most force to move because it was much heavier than the box of cushions. A light object needs less force to make it move than a heavy one.

Crash!

When a moving object hits something that is not moving, a force passes from one object to the other.

THINK about how you play a game of bowling.

- You roll a ball at some bowling pins and try to knock them over.

Does the weight of the ball matter? And what happens if you roll the ball quickly or slowly?

You will need:

10 small plastic bottles ✔

Some water ✔

A strip of paper ✔

A tennis ball ✔

A sponge ball the same size as the tennis ball ✔

What makes the bowling pins fall?

1. Fill each bottle half full of water. These are your bowling pins.

2. Line up the pins on a flat surface and walk five big steps away. Mark this point with the strip of paper. Always stand behind this line to bowl.

3 Roll the tennis ball at the pins and try to knock them over.

4 Now use the sponge ball, rolling it at the same speed as the tennis ball. What is the difference?

5 Try again with each ball, this time rolling them faster.

Because . . .

The tennis ball is much better at knocking over the pins than the sponge ball. This is because when a heavy moving object hits something, it does so with a greater force than a light object moving at the same speed.

THINK about what would happen if you were in the way of a fast-moving car.
● If the car hit you, the force of its movement would knock you over and could even kill you.

Change direction

A force can make a moving object change direction.

THINK about how you ride a bicycle.
- You use a force to turn the handlebars.
- The bicycle changes direction.

How can you make a moving ball change direction?

You will need:

A soft ball ✔

A baseball bat or a racket ✔

A piece of string about 6 feet (2 m) long ✔

Tape ✔

A long pole (e.g. a broom handle) ✔

What makes a moving ball change direction?

1 Start by hitting the ball with the bat and watch how the ball moves.

2 Now tie one end of the string tightly around the ball, as shown.

3 Tie the other end of the string to one end of the pole and tape it in place.

4 Push the other end of the pole firmly into the ground (you might need an adult to help you).

5 Now hit the ball again. What happens this time?

Because . . .

The ball will travel in a straight line until it reaches the end of the string. Then, the force of the string pulling against the moving ball will tug it to one side.

THINK about the ball games that you play. What forces do you use to change the direction of the ball?

Stretch and squash

A force can change the shape of something. A pushing force can squash it, and a pulling force can stretch it.

THINK about what happens when you use your hands to change the shape of something.

How can you change something's shape?

1 Take some clay and make it into different shapes. Think about the actions you used, such as twist, roll, stretch, squeeze.

twist
squeeze

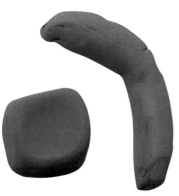

2 List each action, writing next to it if it was a pushing action or a pulling action—or both.

3 Try stretching or squashing the other things you have collected.

4 Make a list of the materials and how you changed their shape, if at all. Write what happened when you let them go.

Because . . .

*The shape of a **material** changes because it is being pushed together or pulled apart. Some things need more force to make them change shape than others.*

Stretching clay needs only a small force, but stretching plastic wrap needs a bigger force. Changing the shape of a block of wood needs a much stronger force than using our hands alone.

*Some materials are bendable and spring back into shape when you let them go. We say they are **elastic**. Elastic materials have a force of their own that brings them back to their original shape when the outside force stops pushing or pulling them.*

Natural forces

There are forces in nature that make things move.

THINK about things that move without people pushing or pulling them.

- A flag on a flagpole flaps.
- Kites swoop around the sky.

What makes them move?

You will need:

A piece of stiff paper or thin cardboard about 6 inches (15 cm) square ✔

A pencil, a ruler, and scissors ✔

2 small beads ✔

A sewing needle ✔

A small wooden stick (e.g. a wooden rod or a pencil) ✔

A small hammer ✔

An adult to help you ✔

What makes a pinwheel whirl?

1. Draw two lines to divide your paper into triangles, as shown. Make a dot on the lines just inside each corner.

2. Inside each triangle, draw a dotted line a half inch (1 cm) to the right of a corner to a half inch (1 cm) below the middle. Cut along these lines.

3 Without creasing the paper, carefully bend each corner into the center so that the corner dots are on top of one another.

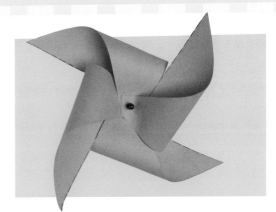

4 Ask an adult to help you thread one bead onto the needle, push the needle through the dots, and then thread the second bead onto the needle on the other side.

5 Now, push the needle into one end of the wooden stick. Your helper may need to tap it in with a hammer. Your pinwheel should move easily if you push it with your finger.

6 What happens when you take your pinwheel outside and hold it up to the wind? What happens if you blow on it?

Because . . .

*Your pinwheel whirls around because the wind pushes air into its sails and makes the wheel spin. Wind can be a very powerful force—think of a **hurricane**!*

Slipping and sticking

Forces make things move, but they can also slow things down. **Friction** is a force that slows things down.

THINK about how things slide across different surfaces.

- Sliding down a slide is easy and fast.
- Sliding down a grassy hill is slow and difficult.

What is the difference between the two surfaces?

You will need:

A small, smooth wooden plank ✔

A test object (e.g. a wooden block) ✔

A pile of books ✔

3 different test surfaces (e.g. felt, sandpaper, shiny plastic) ✔

Tape ✔

A pile of books ✔

A pencil and paper ✔

What difference does a surface make?

(1) Place your test object at one end of the plank. Raise that end until the object starts to slide. Use some books to prop up the plank at that angle.

(2) Tape each of your test surfaces on the plank. How does your test object slide on each surface? Do you have to raise the plank further?

(3) List the surfaces you use, including the wooden surface, and rank the surfaces from one to four (one for the smoothest and four for the roughest). Now rank the slipperiness of the surfaces from one to four. How do their rankings compare?

Because . . .

The smoothest material is also the most slippery. This is because a rough surface produces more friction. Friction is what happens when one object rubs against another. Friction slows things down and stops them from sliding.

THINK about what would happen without friction—every surface would be as slippery as ice.

● How would we walk?
● How would we turn a handle?

Fighting force

Like friction, both air and water push against moving objects and slow them down. This is called **resistance**.

THINK about the ways in which air or water push against you.

- When you paddle in a swimming pool, you feel the water pushing against your body.
- When you walk with your jacket open, you feel air pushing against you. The air is resisting your movement.

How can air and water resistance be useful?

You will need:

A plastic shopping bag ✔

Scissors ✔

Thin string or strong thread ✔

2 identical plastic toy figures ✔

How does air resistance work?

1. Cut a 10-inch (26 cm) square out of the plastic bag.

2. Cut four pieces of string, each about 10 inches (26 cm) long.

3. Make a tiny hole in each corner of the plastic square, about one inch (2 cm) from the edge. Tie a piece of string through each hole in the plastic.

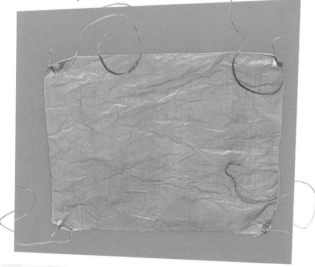

4. Twist the other ends of string together and then tie them around one of the toy figures.

5. Stand on a sturdy chair or table—be careful! First, drop the toy figure that is on its own and count how long it takes to reach the ground.

6. Now, drop the toy with the parachute and count again. Which one takes longer to fall?

Because . . .

The toy with the parachute takes longer to reach the ground because, as it falls, air is trapped underneath the parachute. This air pushes upward against the parachute and slows down the toy's fall.

All fall down

Things fall toward the ground because of a force called **gravity**. Gravity pulls everything toward the center of Earth. Without it, we would all float away into space.

THINK about how gravity pulls things downward.
- When you drop a book, it falls to the ground.
- However high you throw a ball, it always falls back to Earth.

But other forces also affect the pull of gravity on an object.

Think about the parachute test on page 24—then try this experiment.

You will need:
2 sheets of paper ✔
A tennis ball ✔

How does shape affect gravity?

1 Crumple one sheet of paper into a fairly tight ball—it should be about the same size as the tennis ball.

2 Carefully stand on a chair or table. Hold both balls as high as you can. Let them go at exactly the same moment. Which one reaches the ground first?

3 Now, hold the other sheet of paper flat in one hand and the paper ball in the other. Drop them both together. What happens this time?

Because . . .

The two balls hit the ground at the same time. This is because the pull of gravity is the same on both objects. But the flat sheet of paper falls more slowly than the paper ball. This is because the flat paper has a bigger surface, so there is more air resistance to slow it down.

Useful words

Elastic materials stretch and become longer when you pull them but snap back into their original shape when you let go.

Forces make things move, slow down, or change direction. They push or pull on things. You cannot see a force, but you can see what it does and feel how strong it is.

Friction is a force that slows things down. It happens when two surfaces rub together. Rough surfaces create more friction than smooth surfaces. Friction allows us to grip and hold onto things—without it, everything would be slippery.

Gravity is a pulling force. On Earth, gravity is the force that pulls everything toward Earth's center. This is why things always fall downward.

Hurricanes are powerful winds that whirl around in a gigantic circle. They often bring torrential rain and whip up huge waves at sea. Hurricane winds can blow at speeds of more than 124 miles (200 km) per hour and can lift up cars!

Joints are like the hinges on a door—they link all of our bones together and allow our arms, legs, and other body parts to bend.

Cutting resistance

Some things are shaped to reduce air or water resistance. A jet plane's shape helps it move through the air. A dolphin's sleek shape helps it move through water.

Materials can be hard, like metal, or soft, like jelly—or even invisible, like the air we breathe. Everything in the universe is made of some kind of material.

Movement is what happens when something changes its position in some way. Movements can be big, like an aircraft taking off—or very small, like the blink of an eye.

Muscles are the parts of your body that pull on your bones and make them move at the joints. You have more than 600 muscles in your body.

Resistance is what happens when a force pushes or pulls against an object and slows it down. Air and water push against objects moving through them. The faster an object moves, the more air or water will resist it.

Friction makes heat

When two things rub together, the friction between them makes heat. Try rubbing your hands together and feel how friction makes them feel hot.

Gravity on the Moon

The pull of gravity gives things weight. The moon has gravity too, but it is smaller than Earth, so its gravity is weaker. Things weigh less on the moon than they do on Earth. On the moon, an astronaut is six times lighter than he is on Earth, even though his size and shape have not changed.

Index